Alkaline Vegan Diet for Beginners

Easy and Delicious Alkaline Vegan Recipes for Losing Weight, Heal Your Body and Staying Healthy

Elena Peterson

Readers acknowledge that the author is not engaging in the rendering of legal, financial, medical or professional advice.

By reading this document, the reader agrees that under no circumstances are we responsible for any losses, direct or indirect, which are incurred as a result of the use of information contained within this document, including, but not limited to, errors, omissions, or inaccuracies.

Table of contents

CHAPTER 1: WHAT IS AN ALKALINE DIET?

There are many types of diet plans available and are considered to be good or bad depending upon the requirements of the people, but an alkaline diet, without doubt is unanimously considered good for avoiding diseases and remaining healthy.

According to a review published in 2012 in the Journal of Environmental Health, balancing the pH of your body can aid a lot in the reduction of the risk of many chronic diseases like diabetes, hypertension, deficiency of vitamin D, low bone density, arthritis and much more.

An alkaline diet is based on the principle of balancing the blood pH levels of the fluids in your body comprising of both urine and blood. It is also referred to as acid ash diet, alkaline acid diet, alkaline ash diet, at times 'pH diet' and acid alkaline diet. The pH scale of your body is calculated by the amount of minerals in the foods you consume. It is important to know that all living beings and every form of life on earth is surviving on the basis of a certain pH scale and no living being can be harmed by any disease if its pH scale is balanced and in equilibrium.

The tenets of the alkaline diet are based upon the principles from the acid ash hypothesis. As per the research published in Journal of Bone and Mineral Research, grain and protein foods, if consumed in a lower amount, results in the production of net acid excretion (NAE), a diet acid load, release of calcium from bones (skeleton) and increase in urine calcium which leads to osteoporosis which is posited from the acid-ash hypothesis. The alkaline diet is based in such a manner that it avoids osteoporosis by focusing the food pH levels and aims for limiting the risk of dietary acid consumption.

Though expert opinions over this argument might vary but it is unanimously accepted that for the survival of human life, the blood pH level i.e. 7.365–7.4, is very critically important. According to the Forbes Magazine, the human body tries to balance the PH scale at its upmost levels. The pH range of our bodies might be in between 7.35–7.45, depending on our diets, the time of the day and even the time of when we last ate and when we went to the bathroom last time. The reason for an increase in acidosis is referred to the development of electrolyte imbalances and the consumption of acidic foods (acid ash foods) frequently.

What does the "pH level" exactly stands for?

The 'pH' is the short form for potential of hydrogen. It is the value of the either the alkalinity or the acidity of the tissues and fluids of our body. The measurement scale ranges from 0 to 14. The more alkaline a solution is, the higher will be the pH level and the more acidic nature of a solution results in a lower pH value. The balanced and neutral pH level is considered to be 7. It is important to understand that the pH of our bodies is approximately near 7.4, so the appropriate and healthiest pH level for us will be considered to be slightly alkaline in nature. Furthermore, the pH level in our body differs in our body, consider stomach; it is the most acidic organ of our body.

Even a slight change in the pH level of various living beings can result in critical and major complications. Consider an example, the pH level of the oceans has reduced from 8.2 to 8.1 and has caused harmful impacts on the marine lives on a bigger scale due to the rapidly increase in carbon dioxide deposition. The mineral content of the plant related foods is also dependent on the pH levels and can alter it significantly. Minerals, be it in human bodies, soil or even the oceans, are considered to be the reason for buffering the required optimal value of pH levels. It means that any increase in acidity results in lowering the mineral content.

Understand the working of Alkaline

Let us give you a background about the alkalinity/acidity in the human diet along with the pivotal aspects about the working of an alkaline diet.

According to researchers, taking into consideration the net acid load present in the human diet, a considerable and significant change can be noted from hunter gather civilizations to the present human world we live in. The potassium, chloride and magnesium content of the food we eat have significantly dropped with an increase in sodium content as compared to the pre agricultural and industrial revolution times i.e. since the past 200 years.

In normal conditions, the kidney is responsible for marinating the electrolyte levels i.e. magnesium, calcium, sodium and potassium levels. These electrolytes are responsible for countering the acidity if we get exposure to highly acidic substances.

As per the review (mentioned above) from the Journal of Environmental Health, there is drastic change in the potassium to sodium ratio in the diets of many people. Previously potassium was higher as compared to sodium i.e. 10:1, but presently the ratio has drastically changed to 1:3. It means that consumption of sodium is thrice that of potassium on an average for those people who eat the "Standard American Diet".

The diet which mostly adults and children are consuming these days comprises not only of high sodium content with low contents not solely of magnesium or potassium but also low in essential contents like necessary vitamins, fibers and antioxidants. In addition to this, the standard "western" diet comprises of high simple sugar, refined fat, chloride and sodium contents.

All of these alterations in the human diets have caused a considerable increase in a phenomenon called 'metabolic acidosis.' In simpler words, it means that the pH levels of many people are changed from their optimal values. In addition to this, many people are suffering through problems related to magnesium and potassium deficiency along with a low intake of nutrients.

These factors speed up the process of aging, results in a gradual decrease in the efficiency of organs, and degenerates the bone and tissue mass. The high levels of acidity results in robbing off minerals form cells, bones, tissues and organs by our bodies.

How to effectively balance acid foods with alkaline foods?

There are numerous reasons which affect the pH level in the body but the easiest and convenient way is to maintain acid-alkaline equilibrium via your diet. Consuming alkaline foods and reducing acidic foods can help you maintain the acid-alkaline in an efficient way. Alkaline foods are usually plant-based and high in antioxidants, minerals and vitamins. They are easily digestible than acidic foods, improves immune system, reduces inflammation and production of mucus.

The Benefits of Alkaline Diet:

1. **Protects Muscle Mass and Bone Density:**

   The mineral intake plays a crucial and pivotal role in maintaining and developing the structure of bones. According to medical and scientific researches, the higher consumption of alkaline fruits and veggies, the better will be the defense against sarcopenia i.e. the decrease in strength of bones and wasting of muscles with aging.

   The alkaline diet aids and assist in balancing the ratio of critically important minerals for maintain the mass of lean muscles and building bones strong. These minerals include magnesium, phosphate and calcium. Alkaline diets also help a lot in improving producing growth hormones and the absorption of vitamin D. These factors furthermore play a role in protecting bones alongside reducing the risk of many chronic medical ailments.

2. **Reduces the Risk of Strokes & Hypertension:**

The effects of an alkaline diet in anti-aging perspective are considered to be the fact that it stimulates the growth of hormones and reduces inflammation. This is known to improvements in cardiovascular health and plays a defensive role against common medical issues like kidney stones, hypertension which is referred to high blood pressure, stroke, memory loss and high cholesterol.

3. Reduces Inflammation and Chronic Pain:

   According to various studies, there is a direct connection between alkaline diets and the lowered levels of chronic pain. Headaches, chronic back pains, menstrual indicators, joint pain, muscle spasms and inflammation.

   A study conducted by the Society for Minerals and Trace Elements in Germany gave alkaline supplements for a month to patients suffering from chronic back pain. The results showed that 76 out of 82 patients showed a drastic decrement in the pain according to the "Arhus low back pain rating scale."

4. Prevents Magnesium Deficiency and Enhances Vitamin Absorption:

   An increment in magnesium content is necessary for the proper functioning of many bodily processes and enzyme systems. The deficiency of magnesium leads to muscle pains, cardiac complications, sleep issues, anxiety and headaches. Magnesium is also important for activating vitamin D and also preventing its deficiency. It is important to understand that vitamin D is critically important for endocrine functioning and the overall immune system.

5. Lowers Risk of Cancer and Boosts Immune Function:

   The whole body suffers if our cells are low on the required minerals to efficiently oxygenate or dispose of waste from the body. The immune system gets weaker by the accumulation of pathogens and toxins while mineral loss results into compromising vitamin absorption.

According to a study published in the British Journal of Radiology, the process of apoptosis (death of cancerous cells) is more likely to happen in an alkaline body. An alkaline shift in pH scale caused by changes in electric charges and releasing of basic protein components is linked to the prevention of cancer. An alkaline diet can lower the risk of cancer and reduce inflammation. It is also known to be efficient for certain chemotherapeutic agents which need a higher pH level for efficient working.

6. Aids in Having a Healthy Weight:

Consuming more alkaline and less acidic foods aids in protecting you from getting obese resulted by a decrease in inflammation and leptins which affects fat-burning and hunger. Alkaline foods reduce inflammation and that's why it helps you in maintain normal levels of leptin alongside keeping you satisfied on just consuming the required calories.

CHAPTER2: THE VEGAN DIET

What is the Vegan Diet?

A diet only comprising of plant-based foods while restricting the consumption of animal's meat or even their by-products is called a 'vegan diet'. It is a pivotal decision for a person to become a vegan as it completely changes your diet plan and behaviors for the rest of his life.

The reasons for becoming a vegan may range from ethical reasoning of animal harming, religious beliefs and even the effects of the food industry on the eco system. Irrespective of the reasons of conversion, becoming a vegan means letting go of your past food preferences and adopting new ones. It's hard in the starting but not impossible to accomplish at all.

Vegan vs. Vegetarian

Veganism ad vegetarianism gave considerable differences in between them which drastically affect the food plan and choices of an individual.

Vegans only consume foods which are plant based while they avoid anything which is directly or indirectly linked to animals like eggs, milk etc. On the other hand, vegetarians consume plant based food while they avoid meats but they continue consuming the by-products of animals like dairy and eggs etc.

It is easy for vegetarians to achieve their requirements of necessary nutrients like they can easily go for milk as a calcium source while vegans have to find a pure plant-based alternative for calcium intake.

Unlike vegetarians, vegans are strict about not consuming or using anything which has any animal or their by-product or even if any animal or their by-products were utilized in the production of any product. These products include clothes, soaps etc. Recent study in the

US showed that 2.5% of its population is following a vegan diet. Conclusively, veganism is a proper code of life ranging from your food choice to the items you use for domestic purposes while vegetarianism is a pure diet related thing.

Benefits

The benefits of a vegan diet are as follows:

- Limits the risk of type-2 diabetes, certain types of cancer which includes colorectal and prostate cancer and cardiac diseases.
- Improved bone health.
- Aids in blood pressure controlling.
- Limits mortality rate.
- Lowers intake of saturated fats.
- Assists in reducing cholesterol levels.

What is a successful 'Vegan' diet?

The vegan diet is not just about removing meat from your diet plan. It requires eating a properly balanced and nutritious diet. Although veggies and fruits are very beneficial foods but there are certain nutrients present in animals which cannot be easily replaced by a plant-based alternative. To overcome this issue, formulate a healthy, nutritious and balanced diet plan to limit the risk of malnutrition. The most popular replacements for nutrients found in animals are tofu, tempeh and mushrooms. For avoiding malnutrition on a vegan plan, the required intake of the following nutrients should be ensured.

Iron:

It is an important nutrient for producing red blood cells which carry oxygen in the body. Foods rich in iron content are wheat, tofu etc. Broccoli and oranges should also be consumed which are rich in vitamin C.

Protein:

It helps in maintaining skin, bones and other organs healthy. Peanut butter, grains, nuts, seeds, soymilk, tofu, legumes should be consumed for protein intake.

Calcium:

Osteoporosis can be avoided by high consumption of calcium as it makes our bones stronger. Soybeans, almonds, leafy green like bok choy, collard greens and kale can be used as a calcium source for vegans. In addition to these, there are calcium supplements available in market but do check if they fall into the vegan category.

Vitamin D:

It boosts calcium absorption and bone strength. For effective vitamin D production, 10 minutes of exposure to sunlight twice or thrice a day will be enough normally. In case your body requires more vitamin D, you can go for consuming certain cereals and soymilk.

Vitamin B-12:

It assists in the production of red blood cells and in the prevention of anemia. It can be found in fortified products like certain cereals and soymilk and can be consumed for maintain your vitamin B-12 content.

Zinc:

It helps in strengthening the immune system. You can consume beans, nuts and soy related products to maintain your zinc content.

Omega-3 fatty acids:

It improves the efficiency of heart and brain. The most popular sources are flaxseed meal and oil. It can be also found in fortified products with these nutrients from a plant-based source.

CHAPTER3: THE ALKALINE VEGAN DIET

The alkaline vegan diet comprises of those foods which are solely plant based, doesn't come directly or indirectly from animals and are having a pH value above 7. It purely includes alkaline veggies and other plant-based foods while avoiding anything directly or indirectly linked to animals alongside any acidic food.

CHAPTER4: FOODS TO EAT

Following foods are recommended for high consumption:

- Arugula
- Artichokes
- Asparagus
- Baking soda
- Avocado
- Broccoli
- Beets
- Carrots
- Cabbage
- Celery
- Cauliflower
- Chard
- Celery root
- Chives
- Chicory
- Cilantro
- Cucumbers
- Collards
- Dandelion greens
- Fennel
- Eggplant
- Garlic
- Grass (barley grass, wheat grass, kamut grass)

- Green beans
- Ginger
- Jicama
- Leeks
- Kelp (sea veggies)
- Lima beans
- Lettuce
- Lime
- Onions
- Mustard greens
- Parsley
- Peppers
- Peas
- Pumpkin
- Rhubarb
- Radishes
- Sea salt
- Soy beans
- Seaweed
- Spinach
- Soy nuts
- Sprouts (grains, seeds and sprouted beans)
- Sweet potatoes
- Squash
- Tomatoes
- Taro root

- Wasabi

- Turnips

- Watercress

- Green drinks (raw juice with the greens mentioned above)

- Zucchini

CHAPTER5: FOODS NOT TO EAT

Following foods should be eaten in lower quantity (if necessary) are not recommended for consumption:

- Candy
- Alcohol
- Black Tea &Coffee
- Dried Fruit
- Dessert (stating generally)
- Honey
- Sweetened Fruit Juice
- Jam
- Hydrogenated oil
- Jelly
- Dairy and Meat (eggs not as acidic)
- Oatmeal
- Mustard
- Soda
- Sugar, Artificial Sweeteners and Syrups
- Soy Sauce
- Yeast

CHAPTER6: TIPS FOR ALKALINE VEGAN DIET USERS

Following are some important tips for alkaline diet followers:

1. Consume more fruits and veggies.

2. Lower the intake of soda or cut it off altogether.

3. Go for gourds and roots instead of refined carbs.

4. Introduce lime and fresh lemons to your water. Although citrus fruits are generally considered as acidic instead they are highly alkalizing in the body especially limes.

5. Try cooking with sea veggies.

6. Daily consume 64oz of highly-mineral spring water.

7. Increase your protein sources which are plant-based.

8. Introduce ginger, cinnamon and other spices and herbs.

9. Keep a track of your urine pH level. Monitor the pH of your first morning urine after having a sleep of 6 hours approximately to understand the effects of nutritional changes in your body. If the pH result is between 7.5 (somewhat alkaline) and 6.5 (somewhat acidic), it suggests that your overall pH level is at its optimal value i.e. slightly alkaline.

CHAPTER7: FREQUENTLY ASKED QUESTIONS (FAQS)

1. Do acidic foods speeds up the aging process?

    Yes, acidic foods are credited to speed up the aging process. It lowers the growth of hormones.

2. Which calculation procedure for measuring pH is most accurate?

    The most accurate procedure for calculating pH is blood analysis. Although it is less practical and les doable, still it is considered as the most accurate method to measure the pH levels of the body.

3. How does low-grade metabolic acidosis affect us?

    Stating briefly, there are numerous effects of low grade metabolic acidosis on our bodies. These include:

    *   Decreased muscle and bone mass in adults
    *   Growth retardation in children
    *   Kidney stone formation.

The antecedents of low-grade metabolic acidosis are processed foods, animal proteins and sweeteners intake in addition to exposure to pollutants and chronic stress.

CHAPTER 8: BREAKFAST RECIPES

Special Alkaline Breakfast Juice

Preparation Time: 10 minutes

Cooking Time: 0 minute

Servings: 4

Ingredients:

- 2 large carrots, peeled and sliced
- ½ teaspoon fresh ginger
- 4 oranges, peeled and seeded
- 4 celery stalks, chopped
- 3 cups alkaline water

Method:

1. Put the carrots in a blender and add all other ingredients.
2. Blend until smooth and pour into glasses to serve.

Nutritional Value:

- *Calories 105*
- *Total Fat 0.3 g*
- *Saturated Fat 0 g*
- *Cholesterol 0 mg*
- *Total Carbs 25.8 g*
- *Dietary Fiber 5.6 g*
- *Sugar 19.2 g*
- *Protein 2.2 g*

Tofu and Veggie Scramble

Preparation Time: 10 minutes

Cooking Time: 15 minutes

Servings: 4

Ingredients:

- 2 small onions, finely chopped
- 2 cups cherry tomatoes, finely chopped
- 1/8 teaspoon ground turmeric
- 1 tablespoon olive oil
- 2 small red bell peppers, seeded and finely chopped
- 3 cups firm tofu, crumbled and chopped
- 1/8 teaspoon cayenne pepper
- 2 tablespoons fresh basil leaves, chopped
- Salt, to taste

Method:

1. Heat oil in a skillet on medium heat and add onions and bell peppers.
2. Sauté for about 5 minutes and add tomatoes.
3. Cook for about 2 minutes and add tofu, turmeric, cayenne pepper and salt.
4. Cook for about 8 minutes and garnish with basil leaves to serve.

Nutritional Value:

- *Calories 212*
- *Total Fat 11.8 g*
- *Saturated Fat 2.2 g*
- *Cholesterol 0 mg*
- *Total Carbs 14.6 g*
- *Dietary Fiber 4.4 g*
- *Sugar 8 g g*

Fruity Nutty Milkshake

Preparation Time: 10 minutes

Cooking Time: 0 minute

Servings: 4

Ingredients:

- 4 medium mangoes, peeled, pitted and chopped
- 1 cup almonds, chopped
- ½ cup ice cubes
- 3 cups unsweetened almond milk
- 4 medium bananas, peeled and sliced
- 1 teaspoon vanilla extract

Method:

1. Put all the ingredients in a high-speed blender and blend until smooth.
2. Pour into four glasses to serve immediately.

Nutritional Value:

- *Calories 350*
- *Total Fat 15.4 g*
- *Saturated Fat 1.4 g*
- *Cholesterol 0 mg*
- *Total Carbs 52.2 g*
- *Dietary Fiber 8.8 g*
- *Sugar 32.5 g*
- *Protein 8.1 g*

Spiced Quinoa Porridge

Preparation Time: 10 minutes

Cooking Time: 15 minutes

Servings: 2

Ingredients:

- 1 medium mango, peeled, pitted and chopped
- ¼ cup almonds, chopped
- ¼ cup ice cubes
- ¾ cup unsweetened almond milk
- 1 medium banana, peeled and sliced
- ¼ teaspoon vanilla extract

Method:

1. Put mango with rest of the ingredients in a high-speed blender and pulse until smooth.
2. Serve in two glasses.

Nutritional Value:

- *Calories 187*
- *Total Fat 7.8 g*
- *Saturated Fat 0.7 g*
- *Cholesterol 0 mg*
- *Total Carbs 29.2 g*
- *Dietary Fiber 4.7 g*
- *Sugar 19.1 g*
- *Protein 4.2 g*

Avocado Veggie Smoothie

Preparation Time: 10 minutes

Cooking Time: 0 minute

Servings: 4

Ingredients:

- 2 large cucumbers, peeled and chopped
- 2 small green bell peppers, seeded and chopped
- 4 tablespoons fresh lime juice
- 2 cups alkaline water
- 2 medium avocados, peeled, pitted and chopped
- 4 fresh tomatoes, chopped
- 2 cups fresh spinach, torn
- 4 tablespoons homemade vegetable broth

Method:

1. Put all the ingredients in a high-speed blender and pulse till smooth.
2. Pour into four glasses and immediately serve.

Nutritional Value:

- Calories 181
- Total Fat 10.4 g
- Saturated Fat 2.2 g
- Cholesterol 0 mg
- Total Carbs 23.5 g
- Dietary Fiber 7 g
- Sugar 9.9 g
- Protein 4.2 g

Almond and Banana Barley Meal

Preparation Time: 15 minutes

Cooking Time: 5 minutes

Servings: 2

Ingredients:

- 1 cup unsweetened almond milk, divided
- 1 small banana, peeled and sliced
- ½ cup barley
- 3 drops liquid stevia
- ¼ cup almonds, chopped

Method:

1. Put barley, half almond milk and stevia in a bowl and mix well.
2. Cover and refrigerate for about 6 hours and remove from refrigerator.
3. Transfer the barley mixture into a saucepan and add rest of the almond milk.
4. Cook for about 5 minutes on medium heat and dish out in serving bowls.
5. Top with chopped almonds and banana slices to serve.

Nutritional Value:

- *Calories 159*
- *Total Fat 8.4 g*
- *Saturated Fat 0.7 g*
- *Cholesterol 0 mg*
- *Total Carbs 19.8 g*
- *Dietary Fiber 4.1 g*
- *Sugar 6.7 g*
- *Protein 4.6 g*

Rosemary and Sweet Potato Waffles

Preparation Time: 10 minutes

Cooking Time: 10 minutes

Servings: 4

Ingredients:

- 1 teaspoon dried rosemary, crushed
- 2 medium sweet potatoes, peeled, grated and squeezed
- ¼ teaspoon red pepper flakes, crushed
- Salt, to taste

Method:

1. Preheat the waffle iron and grease lightly with cooking spray.
2. Put all the ingredients in a large bowl and mix well.
3. Put half of the potato mixture into preheated waffle iron and cook for about 10 minutes.
4. Repeat with the remaining mixture and serve.

Nutritional Value:

- *Calories 90*
- *Total Fat 0.2 g*
- *Saturated Fat 0.1 g*
- *Cholesterol 0 mg*
- *Total Carbs 21.2 g*
- *Dietary Fiber 3.2 g*
- *Sugar 0.4 g*
- *Protein 1.2 g*

Blueberry Millet Porridge

Preparation Time: 10 minutes

Cooking Time: 20 minutes

Servings: 2

Ingredients:

- Pinch of sea salt
- 1 tablespoon almonds, chopped finely
- ½ cup unsweetened almond milk
- ½ cup millet, rinsed and drained
- 1½ cups alkaline water
- 3 drops liquid stevia
- 1 tablespoon fresh blueberries

Method:

1. Put millet in a non-stick pan on medium-low heat and sauté for about 3 minutes, continuously stirring.
2. Add water and salt and bring to a boil on medium heat and cook for about 15 minutes.
3. Stir in stevia, almonds and almond milk and cook for about 5 more minutes.
4. Layer with blueberries and serve immediately.

Nutritional Value:

- *Calories 219*
- *Total Fat 4.5 g*
- *Total Carbs 38.2 g*
- *Dietary Fiber 5 g*
- *Sugar 0.6 g*
- *Protein 6.4 g*

Zucchini Pancakes

Preparation Time: 15 minutes

Cooking Time: 8 minutes

Servings: 8

Ingredients:

- 12 tablespoons alkaline water
- 6 large zucchinis, grated
- Sea salt, to taste
- 4 tablespoons ground flax Seeds
- 2 teaspoons olive oil
- 2 jalapeño peppers, finely chopped
- ½ cup scallions, finely chopped

Method:

1. Mix together water and flax seeds in a bowl and keep aside.
2. Heat oil in a large non-stick skillet on medium heat and add zucchini, salt and black pepper.
3. Cook for about 3 minutes and transfer the zucchini into a large bowl.
4. Stir in scallions and flax seed mixture and thoroughly mix.
5. Preheat a griddle and grease it lightly with cooking spray.
6. Pour about ¼ of the zucchini mixture into preheated griddle and cook for about 3 minutes.
7. Flip the side carefully and cook for about 2 more minutes.
8. Repeat with the remaining mixture in batches and serve.

Nutritional Value:

- *Calories 71*
- *Total Fat 2.8 g*

- *Saturated Fat 0.4 g*
- *Cholesterol 0 mg*
- *Total Carbs 9.8 g*
- *Dietary Fiber 3.9 g*
- *Sugar 4.5 g*
- *Protein 3.7 g*

Veggie Hash

Preparation Time: 15 minutes

Cooking Time: 20 minutes

Servings: 8

Ingredients:

- 1 orange bell pepper, seeded and chopped
- 1 yellow bell pepper, seeded and chopped
- 1 medium red onion, chopped
- 4 tablespoons fresh parsley, chopped
- 2 tablespoons alkaline water
- Salt and ground black pepper, to taste
- 1 green bell pepper, seeded and chopped
- 1 red bell pepper, seeded and chopped
- 1 tablespoon olive oil
- 1 jalapeño pepper, seeded and chopped
- ¼ teaspoon ground cumin

Method:

1. Put olive oil in a non-stick skillet on medium heat and add onions.
2. Cook for about 3 minutes and add cumin and jalapeno pepper.
3. Cook for about 1 minute and add green bell pepper, orange bell pepper, red bell pepper and yellow bell pepper.
4. Cook for about 3 minutes and season with salt and black pepper.
5. Lock the lid and cook for 15 minutes over medium heat.
6. Dish out and serve hot.

Nutritional Value:

- *Calories 41*

- Total Fat 2 g
- Saturated Fat 0.3 g
- Cholesterol 0 mg
- Total Carbs 6 g
- Dietary Fiber 1.2 g
- Sugar 3.7 g
- Protein 0.8 g

CHAPTER 9: SNACKS AND SIDES RECIPES

Grilled Watermelon

Preparation Time: 10 minutes

Cooking Time: 4 minutes

Servings: 5

Ingredients:

- 1 tablespoon fresh lime juice
- Pinch of cayenne pepper
- ½ watermelon, peeled and cut into 1-inch thick wedges
- 1 garlic clove, finely minced
- Pinch of sea salt

Method:

1. Preheat the grill to high and grease the grill grate.
2. Grill the watermelon pieces for about 2 minutes on each side.
3. Meanwhile, mix together rest of the ingredients in a small bowl.
4. Drizzle the lemon mixture over watermelon slices and serve.

Nutritional Value:

- *Calories 7*
- *Total Fat 0 g*
- *Saturated Fat 0 g*
- *Cholesterol 0 mg*
- *Total Carbs 1.9 g*
- *Dietary Fiber 0.1 g*
- *Sugar 0.9 g*
- *Protein 0.2 g*

Dehydrated Walnuts

Preparation Time: 10 minutes

Cooking Time: 13 hours

Servings: 6

Ingredients:

- 1/8 cup, dates, pitted and mashed into a paste form
- ¼ teaspoon cayenne pepper
- 1½ cups walnuts, soaked for overnight and drained
- ¼ teaspoon ground cinnamon
- Salt, to taste

Method:

1. Mix together all the ingredients in a large mixing bowl and place the walnut mixture over dehydrator sheet.
2. Dehydrate for about 13 hours and serve.

Nutritional Value:

- *Calories 194*
- *Total Fat 18.5 g*
- *Saturated Fat 1.1 g*
- *Cholesterol 0 mg*
- *Total Carbs 3.2 g*
- *Dietary Fiber 2.2 g*
- *Sugar 0.4 g*
- *Protein 7.5 g*

Kale Chips

Preparation Time: 10 minutes

Cooking Time: 15 minutes

Servings: 3

Ingredients:

- ¼ teaspoon cayenne pepper
- ½ tablespoon olive oil
- ½ pound fresh kale leaves, stemmed and torn
- Sea salt, to taste

Method:

1. Preheat the oven to 350 degrees F and line a large baking sheet with a parchment paper.
2. Place kale pieces into prepared baking sheet and sprinkle the kale with salt.
3. Drizzle with olive oil and bake for about 15 minutes.

Nutritional Value:

- *Calories 58*
- *Total Fat 2.4 g*
- *Saturated Fat 0.3 g*
- *Cholesterol 0 mg*
- *Total Carbs 8 g*
- *Dietary Fiber 1.2 g*
- *Sugar 0 g*
- *Protein 2.3 g*

Roasted Spicy Chickpeas

Preparation Time: 10 minutes

Cooking Time: 15 minutes

Servings: 3

Ingredients:

- 1 garlic clove, minced
- 1/8 teaspoon ground cumin
- ¼ teaspoon cayenne pepper
- ½ tablespoon olive oil
- 2 cups cooked chickpeas
- ¼ teaspoon dried oregano, crushed
- ¼ teaspoon smoked paprika
- Sea salt, to taste

Method:

1. Preheat the oven to 400 degrees F and grease a large baking sheet.
2. Layer the chickpeas in the prepared baking sheet and roast for about 30 minutes.
3. Mix together thyme, garlic and spices in a small bowl and take out the baking sheet from oven.
4. Top the chickpeas with oil and garlic mixture and mix to coat well.
5. Roast for 15 more minutes and dish out to serve.

Nutritional Value:

- *Calories 203*
- *Total Fat 5.3 g*
- *Saturated Fat 0.6 g*
- *Cholesterol 0 mg*
- *Total Carbs 30.6 g*

- *Dietary Fiber 8.5 g*
- *Sugar 5.3 g*
- *Protein 9.8 g*

Stuffed Cherry Tomatoes

Preparation Time: 20 minutes

Cooking Time: 0 minute

Servings: 5

Ingredients:

- ½ small avocado, peeled, pitted and chopped
- 1 garlic clove, chopped
- 1 tablespoon fresh basil leaves
- 1½ cups cherry tomatoes
- 1 tablespoon cashews, chopped
- ½ jalapeño pepper, seeded and chopped
- ½ tablespoon fresh lemon juice

Method:

1. Cut the top of each tomato with a sharp knife and remove the seeds from tomatoes with a little scooper to make cups.
2. Transfer the tomatoes in serving plates and place the cut side up.
3. Put rest of the ingredients in a food processor and pulse until smooth.
4. Fill each tomato cup with avocado mixture carefully and immediately serve.

Nutritional Value:

- *Calories 88*
- *Total Fat 5.1 g*
- *Saturated Fat 1.1 g*
- *Cholesterol 0 mg*
- *Total Carbs 10.3 g*
- *Dietary Fiber 3.9 g*
- *Sugar 5.5 g*

Guacamole

Preparation Time: 15 minutes

Cooking Time: 0 minute

Servings: 4

Ingredients:

- ½ small red onion, chopped
- ½ Serrano pepper, seeded and chopped
- 1 tablespoon fresh cilantro leaves, chopped
- 1 tablespoon fresh lime juice
- 1½ medium ripe avocados, peeled, pitted and chopped
- 1 garlic clove, minced
- 1 plum tomato, seeded and chopped
- Salt, to taste

Method:

1. Put avocado in a large bowl and mash completely with a fork.
2. Stir in rest of the ingredients and mix thoroughly to serve.

Nutritional Value:

- *Calories 90*
- *Total Fat 7.3 g*
- *Saturated Fat 1.5 g*
- *Cholesterol 0 mg*
- *Total Carbs 6.5 g*
- *Dietary Fiber 3.1 g*
- *Sugar 1.5 g*
- *Protein 1.2 g*

Cauliflower Hummus

Preparation Time: 10 minutes

Cooking Time: 5 minutes

Servings: 3

Ingredients:

- 1 garlic clove, chopped
- 1 tablespoon olive oil
- Pinch of cayenne pepper
- ½ medium head cauliflower, trimmed and chopped
- 1 tablespoon almond butter
- Sea salt, to taste

Method:

1. Put cauliflower in a large pan of boiling water and cook for about 5 minutes.
2. Drain well and keep aside to slightly cool.
3. Put cauliflower, butter and salt in a food processor and pulse until smooth.
4. Transfer into a serving bowl and sprinkle with cayenne pepper to serve.

Nutritional Value:

- *Calories 98*
- *Total Fat 7.8 g*
- *Saturated Fat 0.9 g*
- *Cholesterol 0 mg*
- *Total Carbs 6.5 g*
- *Dietary Fiber 3 g*
- *Sugar 2.6 g*
- *Protein 3.1 g*

Creamy Green Dip

Preparation Time: 10 minutes

Cooking Time: 0 minute

Servings: 4

Ingredients:

- 1 garlic clove, chopped
- 1/8 cup fresh basil leaves, chopped
- ½ tablespoon fresh lemon juice
- ½ medium avocado, peeled, pitted and chopped
- ½ jalapeño pepper, seeded and chopped
- 1/8 cup fresh spinach, chopped
- Sea salt, to taste

Method:

1. Put all the ingredients in a high-speed blender and pulse until smooth.
2. Serve immediately.

Nutritional Value:

- *Calories 54*
- *Total Fat 4.9 g*
- *Saturated Fat 1.1 g*
- *Cholesterol 0 mg*
- *Total Carbs 2.6 g*
- *Dietary Fiber 1.8 g*
- *Sugar 0.2 g*
- *Protein 0.6 g*

Creamy Blueberry and Avocado Smoothie

Preparation Time: 10 minutes

Cooking Time: 0 minute

Servings: 4

Ingredients:

- 2 cups frozen blueberries
- 4 teaspoons chia seeds
- ½ cup ice cubes
- 2 large avocados, peeled, pitted and chopped
- 3 cups unsweetened almond milk

Method:

1. Put frozen blueberries along with all other ingredients in a high-speed blender and pulse until smooth.
2. Pour into 4 glasses and serve immediately.

Nutritional Value:

- *Calories 311*
- *Total Fat 21.3 g*
- *Saturated Fat 3.2 g*
- *Cholesterol 0 mg*
- *Total Carbs 28.2 g*
- *Dietary Fiber 15.6 g*
- *Sugar 7.5 g*
- *Protein 6.9 g*

Chilled Avocado Soup

Preparation Time: 10 minutes

Cooking Time: 0 minute

Servings: 3

Ingredients:

- ¼ cup fresh cilantro leaves
- 1 tablespoon fresh lemon juice
- 1/8 teaspoon cayenne pepper
- 1½ large avocados, peeled, pitted and chopped
- 1½ cups homemade vegetable broth
- ½ teaspoon ground cumin
- Sea salt, to taste

Method:

1. Put all the ingredients in a high-speed blender and pulse until smooth.
2. Transfer the soup into a large serving bowl and refrigerate for at least 3 hours before serving.

Nutritional Value:

- *Calories 113*
- *Total Fat 9.9 g*
- *Saturated Fat 2.1 g*
- *Cholesterol 0 mg*
- *Total Carbs 6.2 g*
- *Dietary Fiber 4 g*
- *Sugar 1.4 g*
- *Protein 1.1 g*

CHAPTER 10: SALADS RECIPES

Pineapple, Mango Salad with Cranberries and Spinach

Preparation Time: 15 minutes

Cooking Time: 0 minute

Servings: 3

Ingredients:

- ¾ cup mango, peeled, pitted and cubed
- 1/8 cup fresh mint leaves, chopped
- 1 tablespoon fresh orange juice
- ¾ cup fresh pineapple, peeled and chopped
- 3 cups fresh baby spinach
- 1/8 cup dried cranberries
- Sea salt, to taste

Method:

1. Put mango with all other ingredients in a large serving bowl and mix to coat well.
2. Cover and refrigerate for about 3 hours before serving.

Nutritional Value:

- *Calories 59*
- *Total Fat 0.4 g*
- *Saturated Fat 0.1 g*
- *Cholesterol 0 mg*
- *Total Carbs 14 g*
- *Dietary Fiber 2.3 g*
- *Sugar 10.4 g*
- *Protein 1.6 g*

Tomato and Greens Salad

Preparation Time: 15 minutes

Cooking Time: 0 minute

Servings: 6

Ingredients:

- 3 cups cucumbers, sliced
- 3 cups fresh arugula
- 3 tablespoons fresh lime juice
- 3 cups cherry tomatoes, halved
- 3 cups mixed fresh lettuce, torn
- 3 tablespoons extra virgin olive oil
- Sea salt, to taste

Method:

1. Put tomatoes with all other ingredients in a large serving bowl.
2. Toss to coat well and immediately serve.

Nutritional Value:

- *Calories 100*
- *Total Fat 7.3 g*
- *Saturated Fat 1.1 g*
- *Cholesterol 0 mg*
- *Total Carbs 8.6 g*
- *Dietary Fiber 2.1 g*
- *Sugar 4.3 g*
- *Protein 2 g*

Arugula Salad

Preparation Time: 15 minutes

Cooking Time: 0 minute

Servings: 5

Ingredients:

- ½ cup fresh basil, chopped
- 5 cups fresh arugula
- 1½ tablespoons extra-virgin olive oil
- 2 tablespoons apple cider vinegar
- Salt and freshly ground black pepper, to taste

Method:

1. Put olive oil, basil, garlic, vinegar, cracked pepper and salt in an immersion blender and blend until smooth.
2. Combine rest of the ingredients together in a large serving bowl and pour drizzle with dressing.
3. Mix to coat well and immediately serve.

Nutritional Value:

- *Calories 43*
- *Total Fat 4.4 g*
- *Saturated Fat 0.6 g*
- *Cholesterol 0 mg*
- *Total Carbs 0.9 g*
- *Dietary Fiber 0.4 g*
- *Sugar 0.4 g*
- *Protein 0.6 g*

Greens and Pears Salad

Preparation Time: 10 minutes

Cooking Time: 0 minute

Servings: 6

Ingredients:

- 4 tablespoons apple cider vinegar
- 2 tablespoons unsalted cashews
- 8 cups mixed fresh greens
- 2 large green apples, cored and sliced
- Salt and black pepper, to taste

Method:

1. Mix together greens, cashews, apple, salt and black pepper in a large bowl.
2. Top with apple cider vinegar and serve.

Nutritional Value:

- *Calories 179*
- *Total Fat 10.8 g*
- *Saturated Fat 1.6 g*
- *Cholesterol 290 mg*
- *Total Carbs 20.6 g*
- *Dietary Fiber 3.2 g*
- *Sugar 14.6 g*
- *Protein 3.3 g*

Corn and Tomato Salad

Preparation Time: 15 minutes

Cooking Time: 0 minute

Servings: 4

Ingredients:

- 1/8 cup extra virgin olive oil
- 3 cups fresh cherry tomatoes, halved
- 1 tablespoon apple cider vinegar
- 3 tablespoons shallots, minced
- 2 cups corn kernels
- Salt and freshly ground black pepper, to taste

Method:

1. Mix together vinegar, oil, salt and black pepper in a bowl.
2. Add tomatoes and corn and drizzle with dressing mixture.
3. Mix until well coated and immediately serve.

Nutritional Value:

- *Calories 150*
- *Total Fat 7.5 g*
- *Saturated Fat 1.1 g*
- *Cholesterol 0 mg*
- *Total Carbs 21 g*
- *Dietary Fiber 3.7 g*
- *Sugar 6.1 g*
- *Protein 3.9 g*

Beet and Lettuce Salad

Preparation Time: 15 minutes

Cooking Time: 0 minute

Servings: 5

Ingredients:

- 2 tablespoons apple cider vinegar
- 2 tablespoons olive oil
- 6 cups fresh lettuce
- 3 beetroots, chopped
- Salt, to taste

Method:

1. Put fresh lettuce and beetroots in a large serving bowl and drizzle with rest of the ingredients.
2. Toss until well coated and serve.

Nutritional Value:

- *Calories 85*
- *Total Fat 5.8 g*
- *Saturated Fat 0.8 g*
- *Cholesterol 0 mg*
- *Total Carbs 8 g*
- *Dietary Fiber 1.6 g*
- *Sugar 5.5 g*
- *Protein 1.3 g*

Kale Salad

Preparation Time: 15 minutes

Cooking Time: 0 minute

Servings: 4

Ingredients:

- 1½ red onions, sliced
- 2 tablespoons almonds, chopped
- 2 scallions, chopped
- 6 cups fresh kale, trimmed and chopped
- 3 tablespoons fresh orange juice
- 2 tomatoes, sliced
- 1 tablespoon fresh lemon juice

Method:

1. Toss all the ingredients except almonds in a large bowl.
2. Refrigerate to marinate for about 6 hours and top with almonds to serve.

Nutritional Value:

- *Calories 103*
- *Total Fat 1.7 g*
- *Saturated Fat 0.2 g*
- *Cholesterol 0 mg*
- *Total Carbs 19.2 g*
- *Dietary Fiber 3.7 g*
- *Sugar 4.7 g*
- *Protein 4.9 g*

Mango & Bell Pepper Salad

Preparation Time: 15 minutes

Cooking Time: 0 minute

Servings: 5

Ingredients:

For Salad

- 2 mangoes, peeled, pitted and cubed
- 5 cups fresh mixed baby greens
- 1 red bell pepper, seeded and sliced thinly

For Dressing

- 2 tablespoons extra-virgin olive oil
- 1 teaspoon fresh ginger, chopped
- 2 tablespoons apple cider vinegar
- 1 tablespoon fresh cilantro, chopped
- 1 fresh Serrano Chile, chopped
- Salt, to taste

Method:

1. Put all the ingredients for dressing in a blender and pulse until smooth.
2. Combine the mixed baby greens and ¾ of the dressing in a large bowl.
3. Put mango, bell pepper and ¼ of the dressing in another bowl and mix well.
4. Divide the mango mixture and greens onto serving plates and serve.

Nutritional Value:

- *Calories 181*
- *Total Fat 6.3 g*
- *Saturated Fat 0.9 g*
- *Cholesterol 0 mg*

- Total Carbs 30.7 g
- Dietary Fiber 5.5 g
- Sugar 19.6 g
- Protein 4.8 g

Cabbage & Carrot Salad

Preparation Time: 15 minutes

Cooking Time: 0 minute

Servings: 4

Ingredients:

- 2 cups carrot, peeled and shredded
- 2 large scallions, chopped
- 2 tablespoons extra-virgin olive oil
- 1 teaspoon lemon zest, freshly grated
- 2 cups cabbage, shredded
- 1 cup cucumber, sliced
- ½ cup fresh cilantro leaves, chopped
- 2 tablespoons fresh lemon juice

Method:

1. Put all the ingredients in a large serving bowl and toss well to serve.

Nutritional Value:

- *Calories 102*
- *Total Fat 7.2 g*
- *Saturated Fat 1.1 g*
- *Cholesterol 0 mg*
- *Total Carbs 9.6 g*
- *Dietary Fiber 2.8 g*
- *Sugar 4.8 g*
- *Protein 1.4 g*

Olive and Tomato Salad

Preparation Time: 15 minutes

Cooking Time: 0 minute

Servings: 2

Ingredients:

- 1 cucumber, chopped
- ½-ounce green olives, pitted and chopped
- 1/8 cup apple cider vinegar
- 1 large tomato, chopped
- ounce black olives, pitted and halved
- 1/8 red onion, thinly sliced

Method:

1. Mix together all the ingredients except vinegar in a bowl.
2. Drizzle with the vinegar and serve immediately.

Nutritional Value:

- *Calories 67*
- *Total Fat 2.4 g*
- *Saturated Fat 0.4 g*
- *Cholesterol 0 mg*
- *Total Carbs 11.1 g*
- *Dietary Fiber 2.6 g*
- *Sugar 5.3 g*
- *Protein 2.1 g*

CHAPTER 11: MAIN DISHES RECIPES

Stir Fried Spinach and Tofu

Preparation Time: 10 minutes

Cooking Time: 15 minutes

Servings: 4

Ingredients:

- 2 medium onions, chopped
- 3 teaspoons fresh basil, chopped
- 1-pound firm tofu, pressed and cubed
- Sea salt, to taste
- 3 tablespoons olive oil
- 3 garlic cloves, minced
- 1 teaspoon red pepper flakes, crushed
- 6 cups fresh spinach, chopped
- 2 tablespoons fresh lemon juice
- 2 teaspoons white sesame seeds

Method:

1. Heat oil in a pan on medium heat and add onions.
2. Sauté for about 4 minutes and add garlic, basil and red pepper flakes.
3. Sauté for about 1 minute and add tofu.
4. Cook for about 6 minutes and add salt and spinach.
5. Stir fry for about 4 minutes and stir in lemon juice.
6. Remove from heat and garnish with sesame seeds to serve.

Nutritional Value:

- *Calories 214*

- Total Fat 16.1 g
- Saturated Fat 2.6 g
- Cholesterol 0 mg
- Total Carbs 10 g
- Dietary Fiber 3.4 g
- Sugar 3.4 g
- Protein 11.6 g

Green Beans with Quinoa

Preparation Time: 10 minutes

Cooking Time: 20 minutes

Servings: 8

Ingredients:

- 2 small onions, chopped
- 1 teaspoon smoked paprika
- Sea salt, to taste
- 2 pounds fresh green beans, trimmed and cut into 2-inch pieces
- 6 tablespoons olive oil, divided
- 4 garlic cloves, minced
- 2 cups quinoa
- 3 cups homemade vegetable broth
- 4 tablespoons fresh lemon juice

Method:

1. Heat 1 tablespoon of oil in a pan on medium heat and add onions.
2. Sauté for about 3 minutes and add paprika and garlic.
3. Sauté for about 1 minute and add quinoa.
4. Cook for about 1 minute while continuously stirring.
5. Add broth and season with salt and black pepper and bring to a boil.
6. Lower the heat and allow it to simmer for about 15 minutes.
7. Remove from heat and fluff the quinoa with a fork.
8. Add beans in the salted boiling water and cook for about 5 minutes.
9. Mix together green beans and quinoa in a large serving bowl and season with some more salt and black pepper.
10. Drizzle with remaining oil and lemon juice and serve hot.

Nutritional Value:

- *Calories 299*
- *Total Fat 13.3 g*
- *Saturated Fat 1.9 g*
- *Cholesterol 0 mg*
- *Total Carbs 38.9 g*
- *Dietary Fiber 7.8 g*
- *Sugar 3.3 g*
- *Protein 8.5 g*

Roasted Tomatoes with Herbs

Preparation Time: 15 minutes

Cooking Time: 20 minutes

Servings: 3

Ingredients:

- 3 large tomatoes, halved
- 1 tablespoon onion, finely chopped
- ½ jalapeño pepper, seeded and minced
- ½ teaspoon fresh thyme, minced
- 1 tablespoon olive oil
- Sea salt, to taste
- 2 garlic cloves, minced
- ½ tablespoon fresh rosemary, minced
- ½ teaspoon fresh oregano, minced

Method:

1. Line a large plate with paper towel and season the tomatoes evenly with salt.
2. Place tomatoes, cut side down in prepared plate and keep aside for about half an hour.
3. Preheat the oven to 425 degrees F and grease a baking dish.
4. Mix together, onion, garlic, jalapeño pepper and herbs in a small bowl.
5. Place tomatoes, cut side up in a prepared baking dish in a single layer.
6. Top each tomato piece evenly with herb mixture and drizzle generously with oil.
7. Bake for about 20 minutes and serve hot.

Nutritional Value:

- *Calories 81*
- *Total Fat 5.2 g*

- *Saturated Fat 0.8 g*
- *Cholesterol 0 mg*
- *Total Carbs 8.8 g*
- *Dietary Fiber 2.8 g*
- *Sugar 5 g*
- *Protein 1.9 g*

Baked Spicy Zucchini

Preparation Time: 15 minutes

Cooking Time: 20 minutes

Servings: 3

Ingredients:

- ½ small jalapeño pepper, seeded and minced
- 1 tablespoon olive oil
- ¼ teaspoon paprika
- 1 garlic clove, minced
- ¼ cup homemade vegetable broth
- ½ teaspoon ground cumin
- ½ pound zucchini, sliced crosswise
- Sea salt, to taste
- ½ tablespoon fresh lemon juice

Method:

1. Preheat the oven to 400 degrees F.
2. Mix together all ingredients in a large bowl except lemon juice and zucchini.
3. Dredge the zucchini slices in the garlic mixture and transfer them in a shallow baking dish.
4. Pour the remaining mixture evenly over zucchini and cover the baking dish.
5. Bake for about 15 minutes and coat the zucchini slices completely with mixture.
6. Uncover and bake for about 10 more minutes.

Nutritional Value:

- *Calories 58*
- *Total Fat 5 g*
- *Saturated Fat 0.7 g*

- Cholesterol 0 mg
- Total Carbs 3.6 g
- Dietary Fiber 1.1 g
- Sugar 1.7 g
- Protein 1.1 g

Sautéed Brussels Sprouts

Preparation Time: 10 minutes

Cooking Time: 15 minutes

Servings: 4

Ingredients:

- 4 tablespoons olive oil
- 1 teaspoon red pepper flakes, crushed
- 2 tablespoons fresh lemon juice
- 1-pound Brussels sprouts, halved
- 4 garlic cloves, minced
- Sea salt, to taste

Method:

1. Arrange a steamer basket over a large pan of boiling water and place asparagus in it.
2. Cover and steam for about 8 minutes and drain well.
3. Heat oil on medium heat in a large skillet and add garlic and red pepper flakes.
4. Sauté for about 1 minute and add Brussels sprouts and salt.
5. Cook for about 5 minutes and stir in lemon juice.
6. Sauté for about 1 more minute and serve hot.

Nutritional Value:

- *Calories 177*
- *Total Fat 14.6 g*
- *Total Carbs 11.7 g*
- *Dietary Fiber 4.5 g*
- *Sugar 2.7 g*
- *Protein 4.2 g*

Quinoa with Chickpeas & Veggies

Preparation Time: 15 minutes

Cooking Time: 20 minutes

Servings: 3

Ingredients:

- ½ cup quinoa, rinsed
- ½ cup cooked chickpeas
- ½ medium red bell pepper, seeded and chopped
- ¼ cup scallion (green part), chopped
- 1 cup homemade vegetable broth
- Sea salt, to taste
- ½ medium green bell pepper, seeded and chopped
- 1 cucumber, chopped
- ½ tablespoon olive oil
- 1 tablespoon fresh cilantro leaves, chopped

Method:

1. Put broth in a pan and bring to a boil on high heat.
2. Add salt and quinoa and bring to a boil again.
3. Lower the heat and simmer, covered for about 20 minutes.
4. Remove from heat and keep aside for about 10 minutes.
5. Uncover and fluff the quinoa with a fork.
6. Transfer the quinoa in a large serving bowl and stir in the remaining ingredients.

Nutritional Value:

- *Calories 287*
- *Total Fat 6.3 g*
- *Saturated Fat 0.8 g*

- Cholesterol 0 mg

- Total Carbs 46.7 g

- Dietary Fiber 9.4 g

- Sugar 8.1 g

- Protein 11.6 g

Spiced Pumpkin with Beans

Preparation Time: 10 minutes

Cooking Time: 35 minutes

Servings: 2

Ingredients:

- ½ medium onion, chopped
- ½ teaspoon fresh thyme, minced
- ¼ teaspoon ground coriander
- 1 cup fresh tomatoes, chopped finely
- 1 cup homemade vegetable broth
- ½ cup cooked white navy beans
- 1 tablespoon fresh cilantro leaves, chopped
- ½ tablespoon olive oil
- 1 garlic clove, minced
- ½ teaspoon ground cumin
- ½ teaspoon of red pepper flakes
- ½ pound pumpkin, peeled and cubed
- ½ cup cooked red kidney beans
- Sea salt, to taste

Method:

1. Heat oil in a large soup pan on medium heat and add onions.
2. Sauté for about 8 minutes and add garlic, thyme and spices.
3. Sauté for about 1 minute and add tomatoes.
4. Cook for about 3 minutes, crushing with the back of spoon and add pumpkin.
5. Cook for about 3 minutes and add broth.
6. Bring to a boil and reduce the heat to low.

7. Allow to simmer for about 10 minutes and stir in beans.

8. Simmer for 10 more minutes and garnish with cilantro leaves to serve.

Nutritional Value:

- *Calories 320*
- *Total Fat 4.8 g*
- *Saturated Fat 0.8 g*
- *Cholesterol 0 mg*
- *Total Carbs 56.1 g*
- *Dietary Fiber 16.3 g*
- *Sugar 9.3 g*
- *Protein 16.5 g*

Lentils with Kale

Preparation Time: 10 minutes

Cooking Time: 20 minutes

Servings: 3

Ingredients:

- ¾ cup red lentils
- ¼ cup onion, chopped
- 1 garlic clove, minced
- Pinch of crushed red pepper flakes
- 3 cups fresh kale, trimmed and chopped
- Sea salt, to taste
- ¾ cup homemade vegetable broth
- ¾ tablespoon olive oil
- ½ teaspoon fresh ginger, minced
- ¾ cup tomato, chopped

Method:

1. Put lentils and broth in a pan and bring to a boil on medium-high heat.
2. Reduce the heat to low and simmer, covered for about 20 minutes.
3. Remove from heat and keep aside.
4. Heat oil in a large skillet on medium heat and add onions.
5. Sauté for about 6 minutes and add ginger, garlic and red pepper flakes.
6. Sauté for about 1 minute and add tomatoes and kale.
7. Cook for about 5 minutes and stir in lentils and salt.
8. Dish out and serve hot.

Nutritional Value:

- *Calories 251*

- Total Fat 4.2 g

- Saturated Fat 0.6 g

- Cholesterol 0 mg

- Total Carbs 39.8 g

- Dietary Fiber 16.7 g

- Sugar 3.1 g

- Protein 15 g

Chickpeas, Spinach & Carrot Stew

Preparation Time: 15 minutes

Cooking Time: 30 minutes

Servings: 3

Ingredients:

- ½ medium onion, chopped
- 1 garlic clove, minced
- 1 large tomato, peeled, seeded and chopped finely
- 1 cup cooked chickpeas
- ½ tablespoon fresh lemon juice
- ½ tablespoon olive oil
- 1 cup carrots, peeled and chopped
- ½ teaspoon red pepper flakes
- 1 cup homemade vegetable broth
- 1 cup fresh spinach, chopped
- Sea salt, to taste

Method:

1. Heat oil in a large pan on medium heat and add onions and carrots.
2. Sauté for about 7 minutes and add garlic and red pepper flakes.
3. Sauté for about 1 minute and add tomatoes.
4. Cook for about 3 minutes, crushing with the back of spoon and add broth.
5. Bring to a boil and reduce the heat to low.
6. Simmer for about 10 minutes and add chickpeas.
7. Simmer for about 5 minutes and stir in spinach.
8. Simmer for 4 more minutes and stir in lemon juice and salt.
9. Dish out and serve hot.

Nutritional Value:

- Calories 306
- Total Fat 6.6 g
- Saturated Fat 0.8 g
- Cholesterol 0 mg
- Total Carbs 50 g
- Dietary Fiber 14.3 g
- Sugar 12.1 g
- Protein 14.3 g

Roasted Vegetables

Preparation Time: 20 minutes

Cooking Time: 25 minutes

Servings: 4

Ingredients:

- 1½ cups broccoli florets
- 1 tablespoon olive oil
- 1 teaspoon dried thyme, crushed
- ½ teaspoon red pepper flakes, crushed
- 1½ cups cauliflower florets
- 1 cup carrots, peeled and sliced
- 1 tablespoon fresh lemon juice
- Sea salt, to taste

Method:

1. Preheat the oven to 425 degrees F and grease 2 large roasting pans.
2. Put all the ingredients in a large bowl and toss to coat well.
3. Transfer the vegetables into roasting pans and roast for about 25 minutes.

Nutritional Value:

- *Calories 65*
- *Total Fat 3.7 g*
- *Saturated Fat 0.6 g*
- *Cholesterol 0 mg*
- *Total Carbs 7.3 g*
- *Dietary Fiber 2.7 g*
- *Sugar 2.9 g*
- *Protein 2 g*

Vegetarian Chili

Preparation Time: 25 minutes

Cooking Time: 1 hour 10 minutes

Servings: 4

Ingredients:

- ½ medium onion, chopped
- ½ teaspoon ground cumin
- ½ tablespoon red chili powder
- ½ large red bell pepper, seeded and chopped
- 1½ cups tomatoes, chopped
- ¾ cup cooked white beans
- 1/8 cup fresh cilantro leaves, chopped
- 1 tablespoon olive oil
- 2 garlic cloves, minced
- 1/8 teaspoon ground coriander
- Salt, to taste
- 1 medium zucchinis, chopped
- ¾ cup cooked red kidney beans
- 1 cup homemade vegetable broth

Method:

1. Heat oil in a large pan on medium heat and add onions.
2. Sauté for about 9 minutes and add garlic and spices.
3. Sauté for about 1 minute and add garlic and spices.
4. Sauté for about 1 more minute and add all other ingredients except cilantro.
5. Bring to a boil and reduce the heat to low.
6. Allow to simmer for about 1 hour and garnish with cilantro.

Nutritional Value:

- *Calories 351*
- *Total Fat 5.4 g*
- *Saturated Fat 0.9 g*
- *Cholesterol 0 mg*
- *Total Carbs 59 g*
- *Dietary Fiber 15.4 g*
- *Sugar 10.5 g*
- *Protein 21.2 g*

Spicy Vegetables

Preparation Time: 20 minutes

Cooking Time: 25 minutes

Servings: 8

Ingredients:

- 2 large onions, chopped
- 1 teaspoon ground cumin
- ¼ teaspoon ground turmeric
- 4 cups fresh peas, shelled
- 2 cups homemade vegetable broth
- 2 tablespoons fresh lime juice
- 4 tablespoons fresh cilantro leaves, chopped
- 4 tablespoons olive oil
- 4 garlic cloves, minced
- 1 teaspoon cayenne pepper
- 2 pounds cauliflower, cut into florets
- 2 cups homemade tomato puree
- 2 cups fresh green beans, trimmed and cut into 2-inch pieces
- Sea salt, to taste

Method:

1. Heat oil in a large pan on medium heat and add onions.
2. Sauté for about 6 minutes and add garlic and spices.
3. Sauté for about 1 minute and add peas, cauliflower and tomato puree.
4. Cook for about 3 minutes and add broth.
5. Bring to a boil and lower the flame.
6. Simmer, covered for about 10 minutes and stir in green beans.

7. Cook for about 5 minutes and stir in lemon juice and seasoning.

8. Remove from heat and garnish with cilantro leaves to serve.

Nutritional Value:

- Calories 196
- Total Fat 7.6 g
- Saturated Fat 1.1 g
- Cholesterol 0 mg
- Total Carbs 27.5 g
- Dietary Fiber 9.7 g
- Sugar 11.5 g
- Protein 7.8 g

Stir Fried Vegetables

Preparation Time: 20 minutes

Cooking Time: 10 minutes

Servings: 8

Ingredients:

- 8 garlic cloves, minced
- 2 large green bell peppers, seeded and cubed
- 2 large yellow bell peppers, seeded and cubed
- ½ cup homemade vegetable broth
- 4 tablespoons olive oil
- 2 large onions, cubed
- 2 large red bell peppers, seeded and cubed
- 4 cups broccoli florets
- Sea salt, to taste

Method:

1. Heat oil on medium heat in a large skillet and add garlic.
2. Sauté for about 1 minute and add vegetables.
3. Cook for about 5 minutes and add broth.
4. Stir fry for about 4 minutes and dish out.

Nutritional Value:

- *Calories 196*
- *Total Fat 7.6 g*
- *Total Carbs 27.5 g*
- *Dietary Fiber 0.1 g*
- *Sugar 9.7 g*
- *Protein 11.5 g*

CHAPTER 12: SOUPS RECIPES

Mix Vegetables Soup

Preparation Time: 10 minutes

Cooking Time: 45 minutes

Servings: 8

Ingredients:

- 1 medium onion, chopped
- 4 medium carrots, peeled and chopped
- 3 cups small cauliflower florets
- 3 cups small broccoli florets
- 3 tablespoons fresh lemon juice
- 1½ tablespoons olive oil
- 2 celery stalks, chopped
- 2 cups fresh tomatoes, chopped finely
- 3 cups frozen peas
- 8 cups homemade vegetable broth
- Sea salt, to taste

Method:

1. Heat oil on medium heat in a large soup pan and add onions, celery and carrots.
2. Sauté for about 6 minutes and add garlic.
3. Sauté for about 1 minute and add tomatoes.
4. Cook for about 3 minutes, crushing with the back of spoon and add broth and vegetables.
5. Bring to a boil on high heat and lower the heat.
6. Simmer, covered for about 35 minutes and stir in salt and lemon juice.

7. Dish out and serve hot.

Nutritional Value:

- Calories 133
- Total Fat 3.1 g
- Saturated Fat 0.5 g
- Cholesterol 0 mg
- Total Carbs 22.1 g
- Dietary Fiber 7.8 g
- Sugar 9.7 g
- Protein 5.7 g

Greens & Beans Soup

Preparation Time: 10 minutes

Cooking Time: 45 minutes

Servings: 4

Ingredients:

- ½ medium onion, chopped
- 1 medium carrot, peeled and chopped
- 1 tablespoon fresh thyme, minced
- 1½ cups fresh spinach, chopped
- 1 cup white beans, cooked
- 4 cups homemade vegetable broth
- ½ tablespoon olive oil
- 1 celery stalk, chopped
- 1 garlic clove, minced
- 1 cup fresh tomatoes, finely chopped
- 1½ cups fresh kale, trimmed and chopped
- Sea salt, to taste

Method:

1. Heat oil in a large soup pan on medium heat and add onions, celery and carrots.
2. Stir fry for about 6 minutes and add garlic and thyme.
3. Sauté for about 1 minute and add tomatoes.
4. Cook for about 3 minutes, crushing with the back of spoon and add the remaining ingredients.
5. Bring to a boil on high heat and lower the heat.
6. Simmer, covered for about 30 minutes and serve hot.

Nutritional Value:

- Calories 237
- Total Fat 2.4 g
- Saturated Fat 0.4 g
- Cholesterol 0 mg
- Total Carbs 41.8 g
- Dietary Fiber 10.9 g
- Sugar 5.7 g
- Protein 13.7 g

Fresh Green Veggies Soup

Preparation Time: 10 minutes

Cooking Time: 2 minutes

Servings: 4

Ingredients:

- 1 large avocado, peeled, pitted and chopped
- 1 small zucchini, chopped
- ½ small green bell pepper, seeded and chopped
- ½ cup fresh cilantro leaves
- 2 tablespoons fresh lemon juice
- ¼ cup almonds, soaked overnight and drained
- 2 cups fresh spinach leaves
- 2 celery stalks, chopped
- 1½ cups alkaline water
- 2 tablespoons onion, chopped
- 1 garlic clove, chopped
- ¼ cup fresh parsley leaves
- Sea salt, to taste

Method:

1. Put all the ingredients in a high-speed blender and pulse until smooth.
2. Transfer the soup into a pan and cook for about 2 minutes on medium heat.
3. Dish out and serve immediately.

Nutritional Value:

- *Calories 158*
- *Total Fat 13 g*
- *Saturated Fat 2.4 g*

- Cholesterol 0 mg
- Total Carbs 9.7 g
- Dietary Fiber 5.4 g
- Sugar 2.4 g
- Protein 3.5 g

Asparagus Soup

Preparation Time: 10 minutes

Cooking Time: 2 minutes

Servings: 4

Ingredients:

- 3 scallions, chopped
- 4 cups homemade vegetable broth
- Sea salt, to taste
- 1 tablespoon olive oil
- 1½ pounds asparagus, trimmed and chopped
- 2 tablespoons fresh lemon juice

Method:

1. Heat oil in a large pan on medium heat and add scallions.
2. Sauté for about 15 minutes and add asparagus and broth.
3. Bring to a boil and lower the heat.
4. Simmer, covered for about 30 minutes and remove from heat.
5. Transfer the soup into a high-speed blender and pulse until smooth.
6. Return the soup into pan and cook on low heat for about 5 minutes.
7. Stir in salt and lemon juice and serve hot.

Nutritional Value:

- *Calories 108*
- *Total Fat 5.2 g*
- *Total Carbs 8.5 g*
- *Dietary Fiber 3.9 g*
- *Sugar 4.3 g*
- *Protein 8.9 g*

Beet Soup

Preparation Time: 15 minutes

Cooking Time: 1 hour 35 minutes

Servings: 2

Ingredients:

- ½ tablespoon extra-virgin olive oil
- 1 garlic clove, minced
- 1 bay leaf
- Pinch of dried tarragon
- Pinch of ground cinnamon
- 1 large red beet, trimmed
- ½ tablespoon leek, chopped
- ¼ red onion, chopped
- 1 cup vegetable broth
- 1/8 teaspoon dried basil
- 1/8 teaspoon dried oregano
- Pinch of ground cumin
- Salt and black pepper, to taste

Method:

1. Preheat the oven to 360 degrees F.
2. Wrap the beets in a piece of foil and transfer onto a baking sheet.
3. Bake for about 55 minutes and peel and chop the beets.
4. Put oil, leeks and onion in a soup pan and sauté for about 5 minutes.
5. Add bay leaves, garlic, spices and herbs and sauté for about 2 minutes.
6. Add beets and broth and cook for 3 minutes on high heat.
7. Lower the flame and simmer the soup for about 25 minutes.

8. Discard the bay leaves and add soup in a blender in batches.

9. Pulse until smooth and pour the soup back into the pan.

10. Stir in salt and black pepper and cook for about 3 minutes.

11. Dish out and serve hot.

Nutritional Value:

- Calories 82
- Total Fat 4.4 g
- Saturated Fat 0.7 g
- Cholesterol 0 mg
- Total Carbs 7.9 g
- Dietary Fiber 1.6 g
- Sugar 5 g
- Protein 3.6 g

Broccoli Soup

Preparation Time: 15 minutes

Cooking Time: 40 minutes

Servings: 4

Ingredients:

- 1 avocado, peeled, pitted and chopped
- ½ cup onion, chopped
- ¼ teaspoon ground cumin
- 2 medium heads broccoli, cut into florets
- 4 cups vegetable broth, divided
- 1 garlic clove, minced
- 1 tablespoon fresh thyme, chopped
- ¼ teaspoon red pepper flakes, crushed

Method:

1. Heat ½ cup of broth in a large soup pan and add onions.
2. Sauté for about 5 minutes and add spices, thyme and garlic.
3. Sauté for about 2 minutes and add ½ cup of broth and broccoli.
4. Cook for about 3 minutes and add rest of the broth.
5. Reduce the flame and simmer for about 30 minutes.
6. Transfer the soup in a high-speed blender in batches.
7. Pulse until smooth and serve immediately.

Nutritional Value:

- *Calories 166*
- *Total Fat 11.4 g*
- *Saturated Fat 2.5 g*
- *Cholesterol 0 mg*

- Total Carbs 10.4 g
- Dietary Fiber 5.2 g
- Sugar 2.4 g
- Protein 7.4 g

Carrot & Sweet Potato Soup

Preparation Time: 15 minutes

Cooking Time: 10 minutes

Servings: 4

Ingredients:

- ½ cup shallots, chopped
- 2 cups sweet potato, peeled and cubed into ½-inch size
- 4 cups water
- 1 cup carrots, peeled and sliced into ¼-inch size
- 1 teaspoon olive oil
- 1 tablespoon fresh ginger, grated
- 1 teaspoon curry powder
- Salt and black pepper, to taste

Method:

1. Heat oil in a soup pan and add shallots.
2. Sauté for about 3 minutes and add ginger, curry powder, sweet potato, carrot, salt and black pepper.
3. Sauté for about 4 minutes and add water.
4. Let it simmer for about 30 minutes and transfer the soup in a high-speed blender in batches.
5. Pulse until smooth and immediately serve.

Nutritional Value:

- *Calories 132*
- *Total Fat 1.5 g*
- *Saturated Fat 0.2 g*
- *Cholesterol 0 mg*

- Total Carbs 28 g
- Dietary Fiber 4.4 g
- Sugar 7.9 g
- Protein 2.9 g

Peas & Spinach Soup

Preparation Time: 15 minutes

Cooking Time: 20 minutes

Servings: 3

Ingredients:

- 2 chicken bouillon cubes
- 5-ounces frozen onion
- 3 larger celery stalks, chopped
- 2 cups water
- 5-ounce frozen spinach
- Salt and freshly ground black pepper, to taste

Method:

1. Mix together bouillon cubes and water in a large soup pan over medium-high heat and bring to a boil.
2. Add vegetables and bring to a boil again.
3. Lower the heat to medium and cook for about 5 minutes, occasionally stirring.
4. Reduce the heat to low and allow it to simmer for about 15 minutes.
5. Dish out and serve hot.

Nutritional Value:

- *Calories 123*
- *Total Fat 1 g*
- *Saturated Fat 0.3 g*
- *Cholesterol 0 mg*
- *Total Carbs 24.3 g*
- *Dietary Fiber 10.6 g*
- *Sugar 2.3 g*

Carrot & Ginger Soup

Preparation Time: 15 minutes

Cooking Time: 30 minutes

Servings: 4

Ingredients:

- ½ teaspoon vanilla extract
- 1 medium onion chopped
- 1 long red chili, chopped
- 1 tablespoon fresh ginger, peeled and sliced
- 2 cups water
- 3 cups unsweetened almond milk
- 1 tablespoon olive oil
- 2 garlic cloves, minced
- ½ teaspoon fresh turmeric, peeled and sliced
- 4 cups carrots, peeled and chopped
- 2 cups vegetable broth

Method:

1. Heat oil in a large soup pan over medium heat and add onions.
2. Sauté for about 4 minutes and add garlic, red chili and turmeric.
3. Sauté for about 5 minutes and add carrots, water and broth.
4. Bring to a boil and then reduce the heat to low.
5. Simmer for about 20 minutes and remove from heat.
6. Transfer the soup in batches in a high-speed blender and pulse until smooth.
7. Dish out and serve immediately.

Nutritional Value:

- *Calories 149*

- Total Fat 7 g
- Saturated Fat 1 g
- Cholesterol 0 mg
- Total Carbs 18.1 g
- Dietary Fiber 4.5 g
- Sugar 7.7 g
- Protein 4.8 g

Sweet Potatoes & Greens Soup

Preparation Time: 20 minutes

Cooking Time: 35 minutes

Servings: 4

Ingredients:

- ¾ pound sweet potatoes
- 1 tablespoon olive oil
- 1½ carrots, peeled and sliced
- 1½ celery sticks, chopped
- 1 teaspoon fresh ginger, minced
- 1 teaspoon dried thyme
- 1 tablespoon apple cider vinegar
- 2¼ cups water
- Salt and freshly ground black pepper, to taste
- 1 onion, chopped roughly
- 3 garlic cloves, minced
- 1 teaspoon dried rosemary
- 1 teaspoon ground turmeric
- 2 cups low-sodium chicken broth
- 3 cups green leafy vegetables (Swiss chard, kale and spinach), trimmed and chopped

Method:

1. Season chicken evenly with salt and pepper.
2. Heat oil in a large pan and add chicken.
3. Sauté for about 2 minutes on each side and transfer the chicken into a plate.

4. Add carrots, onions, garlic, celery and ginger in the same pan and sauté for about 5 minutes.

5. Add spices and herbs and cook for about 2 minutes.

6. Stir in the vinegar and scrape off the browned bits from the bottom of the pan.

7. Add the chicken pieces and broth and cook, covered for about 20 minutes.

8. Stir in greens and cook for about 4 minutes and serve hot.

Nutritional Value:

- *Calories 191*
- *Total Fat 3.8 g*
- *Saturated Fat 0.6 g*
- *Cholesterol 0 mg*
- *Total Carbs 34 g*
- *Dietary Fiber 8.2 g*
- *Sugar 4.4 g*
- *Protein 6.1 g*

CHAPTER 13: DESSERTS RECIPES

Glazed Banana

Preparation Time: 15 minutes

Cooking Time: 4 minutes

Servings: 4

Ingredients:

- 2 under-ripened bananas, peeled and sliced
- 2 tablespoons applesauce, unsweetened
- 2 tablespoons olive oil
- 2 tablespoons water
- ¼ teaspoon ground cinnamon

Method:

1. Heat oil in a non-stick skillet over medium heat and add banana slices.
2. Cook for about 2 minutes on each side and dish out the banana slices onto a serving plate.
3. Mix applesauce and water in a small bowl and beat well.
4. Pour the applesauce mixture evenly over banana slices and keep aside.
5. Sprinkle cinnamon and serve.

Nutritional Value:

- *Calories 119*
- *Total Fat 7 g*
- *Saturated Fat 1 g*
- *Cholesterol 0 mg*
- *Total Carbs 13.5 g*
- *Dietary Fiber 1.7 g*

- *Sugar 10.8 g*
- *Protein 0.5 g*

Baked Apple

Preparation Time: 10 minutes

Cooking Time: 35 minutes

Servings: 4

Ingredients:

- ¼ teaspoon ground cinnamon
- 2 large apples, cored and cut into 8 slices

Method:

1. Preheat the oven to 400 degrees F and line a baking sheet with parchment paper.
2. Arrange apple slices in prepared baking sheet in a single layer and sprinkle with cinnamon.
3. Bake for about 35 minutes and serve.

Nutritional Value:

- *Calories 58*
- *Total Fat 0.2 g*
- *Saturated Fat 0 g*
- *Cholesterol 0 mg*
- *Total Carbs 15.5 g*
- *Dietary Fiber 2.8 g*
- *Sugar 11.6 g*
- *Protein 0.3 g*

Spinach & Fruit Frozen Treat

Preparation Time: 20 minutes

Cooking Time: 0 minute

Servings: 6

Ingredients:

- 4 frozen ripe bananas, peeled and sliced
- ½ cup frozen pineapple chunks
- 2 teaspoons vanilla extract
- 2½ cups fresh spinach
- 1½ cups frozen mango chunks
- 2 tablespoons unsweetened almond milk

Method:

1. Put all the ingredients in a food processor and pulse until creamy and smooth.
2. Dish out and immediately serve.

Nutritional Value:

- *Calories 120*
- *Total Fat 0.6 g*
- *Saturated Fat 0.2 g*
- *Cholesterol 0 mg*
- *Total Carbs 29.4 g*
- *Dietary Fiber 3.2 g*
- *Sugar 19.8 g*
- *Protein 1.7 g*

Grilled Peaches

Preparation Time: 15 minutes

Cooking Time: 10 minutes

Servings: 6

Ingredients:

- ½ cup coconut cream
- ¼ cup walnuts, chopped
- 3 medium peaches, halved and pitted
- 1 teaspoon vanilla extract
- 1/8 teaspoon ground cinnamon

Method:

1. Preheat the grill to medium-low heat and grease the grill grate.
2. Arrange the peach slices cut-side down onto grate and grill for about 5 minutes on each side.
3. Mix together coconut cream and vanilla extract in a bowl and beat until smooth.
4. Spoon the whipped cream over each peach half and top with walnuts and cinnamon to serve.

Nutritional Value:

- *Calories 110*
- *Total Fat 8 g*
- *Saturated Fat 4.4 g*
- *Cholesterol 0 mg*
- *Total Carbs 8.8 g*
- *Dietary Fiber 2 g*
- *Sugar 7.8 g*
- *Protein 2.4 g*

Pineapple and Banana Frozen Treat

Preparation Time: 10 minutes

Cooking Time: 0 minute

Servings: 3

Ingredients:

- ½ cup frozen pineapple chunks, thawed
- Pinch of salt
- 7-ounce unsweetened almond milk
- 2 cups frozen banana slices, thawed
- 1 tablespoon fresh lime juice

Method:

1. Line a glass baking dish with a plastic wrap and keep aside.
2. Put all the ingredients in a high-speed blender and pulse until smooth.
3. Transfer the mixture evenly into prepared baking dish and freeze for about 40 minutes before serving.

Nutritional Value:

- *Calories 138*
- *Total Fat 1.3 g*
- *Saturated Fat 0.2 g*
- *Cholesterol 0 mg*
- *Total Carbs 33.7 g*
- *Dietary Fiber 3.4 g*
- *Sugar 21.1 g*
- *Protein 1.6 g*

Berry Granita

Preparation Time: 20 minutes

Cooking Time: 0 minute

Servings: 4

Ingredients:

- 1 cup fresh blueberries
- 2 tablespoons unsweetened applesauce
- 2 cups crushed ice
- 2 cups fresh strawberries, hulled and sliced
- 1 cup fresh blackberries
- 2 tablespoons fresh lemon juice

Method:

1. Put all the ingredients in a high-speed blender and pulse until smooth.
2. Transfer the mixture into an 8x8-inch baking dish and freeze for at least 30 minutes.
3. Remove from freezer and stir the granita completely with a fork.
4. Freeze for about 1 hour, scraping after every 30 minutes.

Nutritional Value:

- Calories 64
- Total Fat 0.6 g
- Saturated Fat 0.1 g
- Cholesterol 0 mg
- Total Carbs 15.3 g
- Dietary Fiber 4.4 g
- Sugar 9.8 g
- Protein 1.3 g

Blueberry Fudge

Preparation Time: 20 minutes

Cooking Time: 0 minute

Servings: 16

Ingredients:

- 6-ounce raw cashews
- ½ teaspoon vanilla extract
- ½ cup almond butter, melted
- ¾ cup unsweetened vanilla almond milk
- 4-ounce frozen blueberries
- ½ teaspoon stevia
- 1/8 teaspoon salt
- 1½ scoops vanilla protein powder

Method:

1. Mix together almond milk, cashews and blueberries in a bowl and refrigerate overnight.
2. Put blueberry mixture, both extracts and salt in a high-speed blender and pulse until smooth.
3. Add protein powder and almond butter and pulse until well combined.
4. Transfer the mixture evenly into parchment lined baking dish and smooth the top surface with the back of a spatula.
5. Cover he baking dish with a piece of foil and refrigerate overnight.
6. Cut into desired sized squares and serve immediately.

Nutritional Value:

- *Calories 90*
- *Total Fat 5.8 g*

- Saturated Fat 1.1 g
- Cholesterol 13 mg
- Total Carbs 5.5 g
- Dietary Fiber 0.6 g
- Sugar 1.6 g
- Protein 4.7 g

Pumpkin Pudding

Preparation Time: 20 minutes

Cooking Time: 0 minute

Servings: 8

Ingredients:

- 2 ripe bananas, peeled and sliced
- ½ cup almond butter
- ½ teaspoon ground ginger
- ½ teaspoon salt
- 1½ cup pumpkin puree
- 1 avocado, peeled, pitted and chopped
- ½ cup unsweetened applesauce
- 2 teaspoons ground cinnamon
- ½ teaspoon ground nutmeg
- 2 teaspoons vanilla extract

Method:

1. Put all the ingredients in a food processor and pulse until smooth.
2. Divide pudding into serving bowls and refrigerate for at least 2 hours before serving.

Nutritional Value:

- *Calories 111*
- *Total Fat 5.8 g*
- *Saturated Fat 1.2 g*
- *Cholesterol 0 mg*
- *Total Carbs 15.3 g*
- *Dietary Fiber 4.4 g*

- *Sugar 7 g*
- *Protein 1.6 g*

CONCLUSION

There are many types of diet plans available and are considered to be good or bad depending upon the requirements of the people, but an alkaline diet, without doubt is unanimously considered good for avoiding diseases and remaining healthy. An alkaline diet is based on the principle of balancing the blood pH levels of the fluids in your body including both urine and blood. It is also referred to as acid-ash diet, alkaline acid diet, alkaline-ash diet, at times 'pH diet' and acid alkaline diet. The pH scale of your body is calculated by the amount of minerals in the foods you consume. It is important to know that all living beings and every form of life on earth is surviving on the basis of a certain pH scale and no living being can be harmed by any disease if its pH scale is balanced and in equilibrium.

The alkaline vegan diet comprises of those foods which are solely plant based, doesn't come directly or indirectly from animals and are having a pH value above 7. It purely includes alkaline veggies and other plant based foods while avoiding anything directly or indirectly linked to animals alongside any acidic food.

9 781720 809210